MISSION TO MARS

MARS: THE RED PLANET

BY

JOHN HAMILTON

Abdo & Daughters
An imprint of Abdo Publishing | abdopublishing.com

abdopublishing.com

Published by Abdo Publishing, a division of ABDO, PO Box 398166, Minneapolis, Minnesota 55439. Copyright © 2019 by Abdo Consulting Group, Inc. International copyrights reserved in all countries. No part of this book may be reproduced in any form without written permission from the publisher. Abdo & Daughters™ is a trademark and logo of Abdo Publishing.

Printed in the United States of America, North Mankato, Minnesota.
042018
092018

THIS BOOK CONTAINS
RECYCLED MATERIALS

Editor: Sue Hamilton
Copy Editor: Bridget O'Brien
Graphic Design: Sue Hamilton
Cover Design: Candice Keimig and Pakou Moua
Cover Photo: iStock
Interior Images: All Images NASA, except:
European Space Agency-pgs 15, 26-27, 36 & 45; Getty-pg 38;
Indian Space Research Organization-pg 45; iStock-pgs 10-11 (bottom) & 14;
Lunar and Planetary Institute-pg 13 (top); National Geographic-pgs 6-7;
Shutterstock-pg 37; Wikimedia-pgs 24 (top), 39 & 40.

Library of Congress Control Number: 2017963898
Publisher's Cataloging-in-Publication Data
Names: Hamilton, John, author.
Title: Mars: the red planet / by John Hamilton
Description: Minneapolis, Minnesota : Abdo Publishing, 2019. | Series: Mission to Mars | Includes online resources and index.
Identifiers: ISBN 9781532115974 (lib.bdg.) | ISBN 9781532156908 (ebook)
Subjects: LCSH: Martian geomorphology--Juvenile literature. | Mars (Planet)--Atmosphere--Juvenile literature. | Mars (Planet)--Exploration--Juvenile literature.
Classification: DDC 523.43--dc23

CONTENTS

THE RED PLANET

For thousands of years, people have stared up at the planet Mars and marveled at its mysteries. The blood-red disk in the night sky captured the imagination of writers, poets, and philosophers. The ancient Greeks and Romans believed Mars was the god of war. Its fierce reputation continues to this day. The Red Planet has been the subject of countless science fiction books, stories, and movies. They include *War of the Worlds*, *The Expanse*, and *The Martian*, to name just a few.

Today, Mars is much more than just a frightening object of imagination. It is a real place that we have explored not only with powerful telescopes, but also a fleet of orbiters, landers, and rovers. In just the past two decades, scientists have learned more about Mars than in all of human history combined.

Mars is a place that continues to surprise and inspire. With manned missions planned for the not-too-distant future, we will certainly learn much more about the mysterious Red Planet. Perhaps people will eventually live there in permanent settlements. The science we learn on distant Mars may even someday help us to repair and sustain our own planet Earth. The challenges are many, but the possibilities are endless.

MAPS OF MARS

These maps show the western and eastern hemispheres of Mars. They were created by combining thousands of photos taken by NASA's Mars Global Surveyor, an orbiting satellite that mapped Mars from 1999 to 2006. The maps show the colors that astronauts would see when traveling to Mars.

WESTERN HEMISPHERE

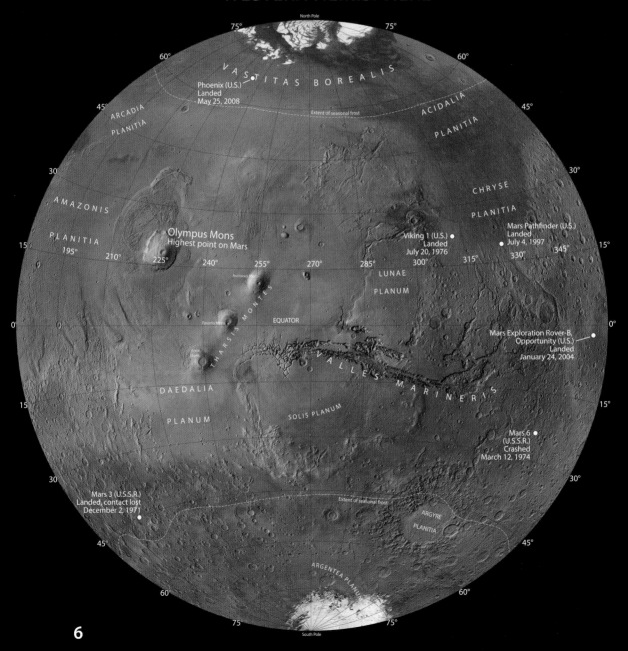

North Pole

75° 75°

60° 60°

VASTITAS BOREALIS

Phoenix (U.S.)
Landed
May 25, 2008

ACIDALIA

45° 45°

Extent of seasonal frost

ARCADIA

PLANITIA

PLANITIA

30° 30°

CHRYSE

PLANITIA

AMAZONIS

Olympus Mons
Highest point on Mars

Mars Pathfinder (U.S.)
Landed
July 4, 1997

PLANITIA

Viking 1 (U.S.)
Landed
July 20, 1976

15° 15°
195° 210° 225° 240° 255° 270° 285° 300° 315° 330° 345°

Ascraeus Mons

LUNAE

PLANUM

Pavonis Mons

EQUATOR

0° 0°

Mars Exploration Rover-B,
Opportunity (U.S.)
Landed
January 24, 2004

Arsia Mons

THARSIS MONTES

VALLES MARINERIS

DAEDALIA

15° 15°

PLANUM

SOLIS PLANUM

Mars 6
(U.S.S.R.)
Crashed
March 12, 1974

30° 30°

Mars 3 (U.S.S.R.)
Landed, contact lost
December 2, 1971

Extent of seasonal frost

ARGYRE

PLANITIA

45° 45°

ARGENTEA PLANUM

60° 60°

75° 75°

South Pole

6

EASTERN HEMISPHERE

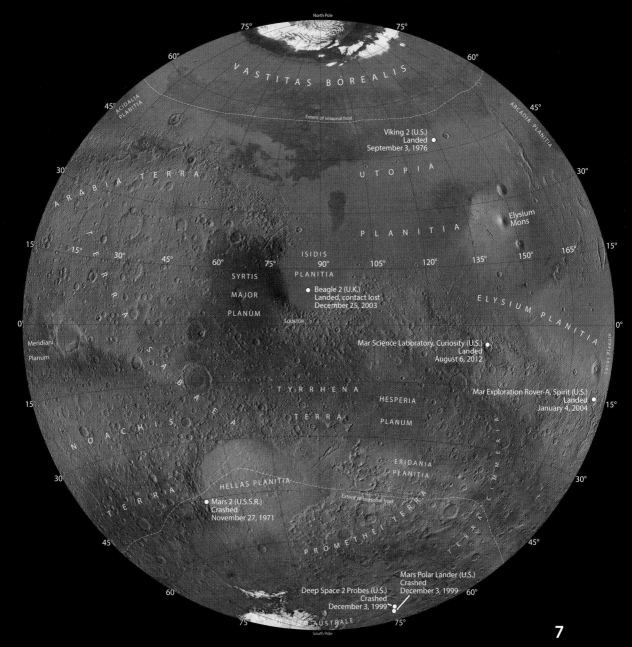

ANCIENT HISTORY

Our solar system formed from a collapsing cloud of interstellar dust and gasses 4.6 billion years ago. About 3.5 billion years ago, Mars and Earth were much more similar than they are today. Both had mild temperatures and oceans of water. We know this because there are geological features on Mars that could only have been formed by water. They include dry riverbeds, deltas, lakes, and ocean basins. There are also layers of sedimentary rocks that need water to exist.

This is an artist's concept of an ancient, habitable Mars capable of supporting liquid water on its surface.

Water is a central ingredient for life to arise. It supports the complex chemical reactions that living things depend on. By the time life began on Earth, it is possible that some sort of life may have already existed on Mars.

Over billions of years, the atmosphere on Mars became thinner and thinner. Eventually, all of the surface water evaporated or froze. There was too little atmospheric pressure for liquid water to exist. Today, Mars is a cold, dry place. It is too harsh for humans to live there unprotected.

ORBIT

Mars is the fourth planet from the Sun. It is the outermost of the four terrestrial planets. The terrestrial planets are rocky and similar in size to Earth. They are also closest to the Sun. The four outer planets of the solar system are gas and ice giants that are much larger than Earth.

A day on Mars (a sol) lasts about 24 hours and 39 minutes. That is not much longer than a day on Earth. Mars orbits the Sun every 687 Earth days. A 15-year-old on Earth would have had only 8 birthdays on Mars.

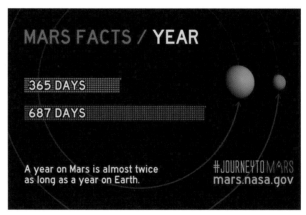

MARS FACTS / **YEAR**

365 DAYS

687 DAYS

A year on Mars is almost twice as long as a year on Earth.

#JOURNEYTOMARS
mars.nasa.gov

If Earth was the size of a dime and it was placed on the goal line of a football field, the Moon would be less than a yard away. Mars would be about the size of an aspirin, and would be on the other goal line during the closest part of its orbit.

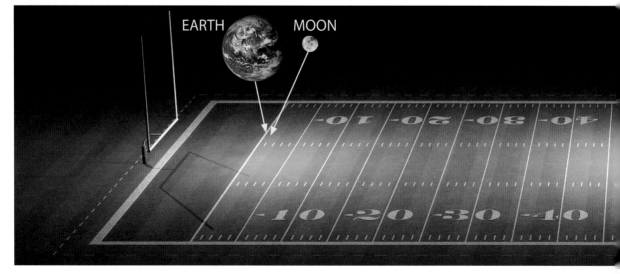

EARTH   MOON

Mars is about 142 million miles (229 million km) from the Sun. By comparison, Earth is 93 million miles (150 million km) from the Sun. The speed of

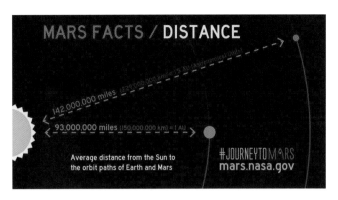

light is 186,000 miles per second (299,338 km/sec). It takes light from the Sun almost 13 minutes to reach Mars. Its greater distance from the Sun is one reason why Mars is so much colder than Earth.

The distance between Mars and Earth is always changing as the planets orbit the Sun. At their closest, they are about 35 million miles (56 million km) apart. That is near enough for Mars to appear as a bright, red object in the night sky. When Earth and Mars are on opposite sides of the Sun, they are about 250 million miles (402 million km) apart. About every 26 months, the planets are lined up properly for spacecraft to travel to Mars. A journey to the Red Planet takes about six to eight months, using current rocket technology.

SIZE AND GRAVITY

Mars is about half the size of Earth. Its diameter (the distance through the planet's center from one side to another) is about 4,220 miles (6,791 km) at its equator. In comparison, Earth's diameter is 7,926 miles (12,756 km).

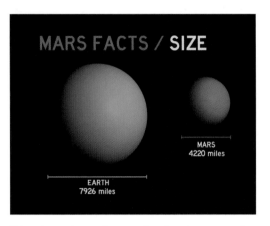

MARS FACTS / SIZE

MARS
4220 miles

EARTH
7926 miles

Mars is not a perfect sphere. Just like Earth, it has a bulge around its equator because it spins, or rotates, around its axis. If measured through the poles, Mars's diameter is slightly shorter, measuring 4,196 miles (6,753 km).

The circumference of Mars (the distance around the equator) is 13,233 miles (21,296 km). The circumference of Earth is 24,874 miles (40,031 km).

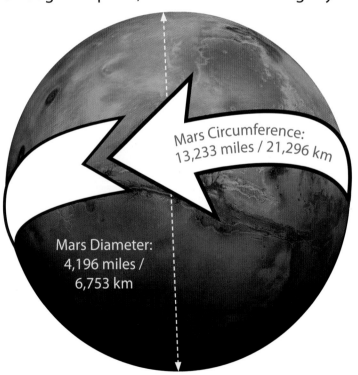

Mars Circumference:
13,233 miles / 21,296 km

Mars Diameter:
4,196 miles /
6,753 km

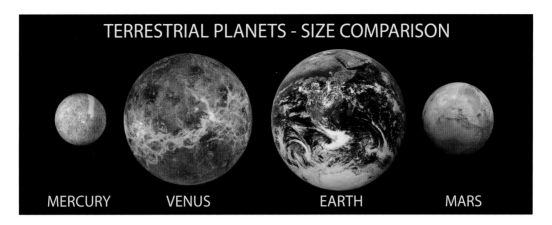

TERRESTRIAL PLANETS - SIZE COMPARISON

MERCURY　　VENUS　　EARTH　　MARS

Mercury is the only planet in our solar system smaller than Mars. (Pluto is a dwarf planet, which is smaller than Earth's Moon.) Mars is smaller than Earth, but it has no liquid oceans. Because of this, its land area is about the same as all the dry land on Earth.

The gravity on Mars is about 38 percent less than on Earth, thanks to the Red Planet's smaller size and density, or mass. A 200-pound (91-kg) astronaut would weigh just 76 pounds (34 kg) on Mars. People walking on Mars would feel lighter on their feet, and just about anyone would be able to dunk a basketball!

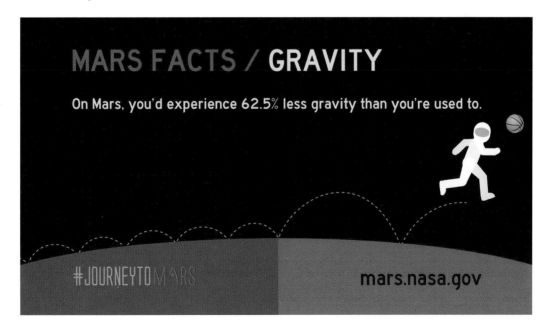

MARS FACTS / GRAVITY

On Mars, you'd experience 62.5% less gravity than you're used to.

#JOURNEYTOMARS　　mars.nasa.gov

WHY IS MARS RED?

From the inky black of the night sky, Mars appears like a glowering red eye staring back at Earth. That is one reason why the planet was so feared by early civilizations, and why Mars became known as the god of war by the ancient Greeks and Romans. The truth behind its blood-red hue, however, is far less sinister.

A color image
of Mars shows
the planet's red glow.

The red color we see from Earth is caused by fine-grained dust. It covers much of the surface of Mars, and in some places is several feet thick. The dust is rich in iron. When exposed to oxygen in the air, the iron rusts (oxidizes) and turns a dull, butterscotch-like color. The oxidized dust is so light that it is easily blown high into the Martian atmosphere. This dust, together with other common rocks on Mars, including grayish volcanic basalt, causes Mars to appear the dull red color we see from Earth.

ATMOSPHERE

M ars has an atmosphere, but it is very thin. Its wispy air is less than one percent as dense as the atmosphere on Earth. That is about as thin as the air at 30,000 feet (9,144 m) above Earth, which is almost as high as passenger airplanes fly. With the air so thin, hurricane-strength winds on Mars would feel like a spring breeze to astronauts.

In its younger days, Mars had a thick atmosphere much like Earth today. That allowed water to collect and pool in oceans, rivers, and lakes. Then, over billions of years, the atmosphere began to disappear. The water evaporated, seeped underground, or froze and collected as ice on the poles.

Solar wind and radiation stripped the Martian atmosphere, transforming Mars from a planet that could have supported life billions of years ago into a frigid desert world. Artwork shows early Mars (near right) may have looked similar to Earth with liquid water and a thicker atmosphere. Today's Mars (far right) is a cold, dry environment.

Most of Mars's remaining atmosphere is carbon dioxide. There are also small amounts of argon, nitrogen, oxygen, carbon monoxide, and water vapor. Trace amounts of methane and ammonia have also been detected.

Because Mars doesn't have a thick atmosphere like Earth, its surface is often struck by asteroids. (Most space debris falling to Earth is burned up in its thick atmosphere.) NASA satellites orbiting Mars have even photographed new craters on the Martian surface.

CLIMATE AND WEATHER

Mars is a very cold planet. On a typical "warm" day, temperatures are like winters in Minnesota or North Dakota. On average, Martian temperatures are similar to what you might find in Antarctica. The planet's average surface temperature is a frigid -81 degrees Fahrenheit (-63 degrees C). However, it can sometimes get down to -225 degrees F (-143 degrees C), or climb as high as 70 degrees F (21 degrees C) on warm summer days near the equator.

Mars is a cold planet for several reasons. It is about one and a half times farther from the Sun than Earth. Also, heat escapes much faster in Mars's thin atmosphere.

BLUE SKIES ON MARS?

During the day, the sky on Mars is rust colored because of all the dust particles floating in the air. Iron oxide in the dust absorbs blue wavelengths, which cause Martian skies to be a dull yellow-brown, butterscotch-like color. Light is also scattered in complex ways. On Mars, there is a blue halo that surrounds the Sun. It is most noticeable during Martian sunsets.

A blue sunset on Mars.

A dust devil swirls across the Amazonis Planitia region of northern Mars. The serpentine winds were photographed from space by NASA's Mars Reconnaissance Orbiter.

Mars is tilted slightly on its axis. As it orbits the Sun, the tilt causes seasons, just like on Earth. The seasons last longer because Mars takes longer to orbit the Sun. During winter, carbon dioxide in the air freezes and collects at the poles. In summer, it evaporates back into the atmosphere. Sometimes frozen carbon dioxide particles form snow, or fog.

Martian winds are sometimes strong enough to create massive dust storms that cover huge parts of the planet's surface. Dust devils also form, which have been seen by orbiting NASA satellites. These whirlwinds often create beautiful, swirling designs in the Martian dust.

GEOLOGY

Mars has a metallic core, much like Earth. Mars's core is made mostly of iron, nickel, and sulfur. The outer part of the core is liquid, made of molten rock. We know this by studying gravity maps. Like doctors peering at an x-ray, the maps help scientists "see" inside Mars. The gravity maps were made over 16 years by a trio of NASA satellites orbiting the planet.

Also like Earth, Mars has a soft, paste-like mantle surrounding the core. It also has an outer crust. The crust averages about 31 miles (50 km) thick. By comparison, Earth's crust averages 25 miles (40 km) thick.

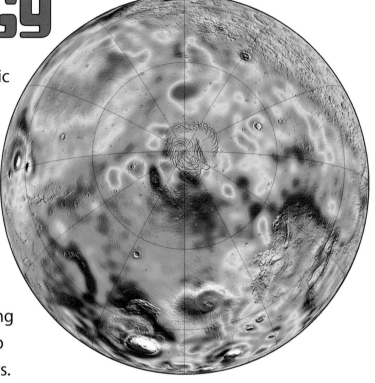

Above: A map of Martian gravity looking down on the North Pole (center). White and red are areas of higher gravity. Blue indicates areas of lower gravity.

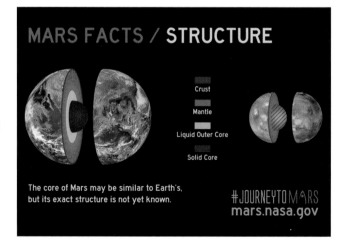

MARS FACTS / **STRUCTURE**

Crust

Mantle

Liquid Outer Core

Solid Core

The core of Mars may be similar to Earth's, but its exact structure is not yet known.

#JOURNEYTOMARS
mars.nasa.gov

Basalt boulders on the red sand surface of Mars were formed by volcanic processes. These basaltic rocks have the same small holes that are found in some of Earth's volcanic rocks.

Earth's crust is broken into huge, continental plates that rub against each other as they float over the mantle. The areas between the plates experience earthquakes and volcanoes. The crust of Mars isn't broken into plates, although it may have been millions of years ago. Large areas of the Martian surface are covered with hardened lava plains. Mars is also home to some of the largest volcanoes in the solar system.

The Martian surface is covered by a layer of talcum powder-like dust containing oxidized (rusted) iron. It is several feet thick in some places. Underneath the dust, Mars's crust contains mostly volcanic basalt rock. The Martian soil contains nutrients such as sodium, potassium, magnesium, and chloride, which are needed to grow plants. Perhaps someday future astronauts will be able to grow crops on Mars.

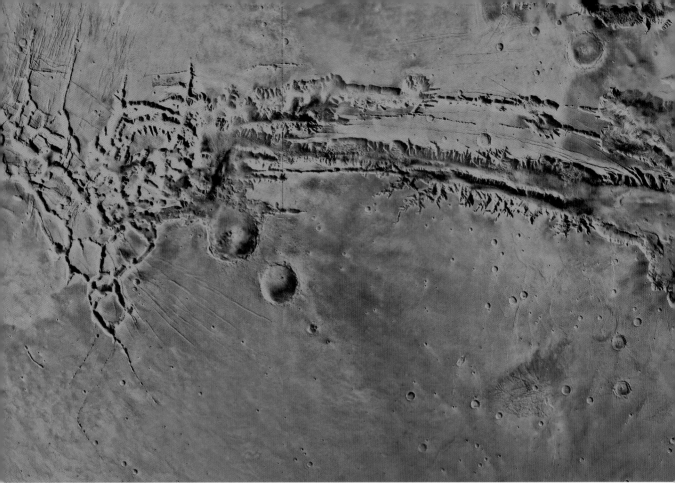

THE GRAND CANYON OF MARS

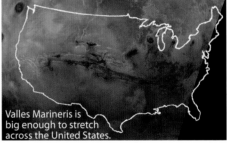

Valles Marineris is big enough to stretch across the United States.

Mars is home to spectacular scenic landscapes. That includes Valles Marineris, the biggest canyon system on Mars. Dwarfing Earth's Grand Canyon, Valles Marineris is one of the largest canyons in the entire solar system. It is located in the southern hemisphere and lies just south of the equator.

Valles Marineris covers almost one-fifth of Mars's circumference. If it was on Earth, it would stretch across the United States from east to west.

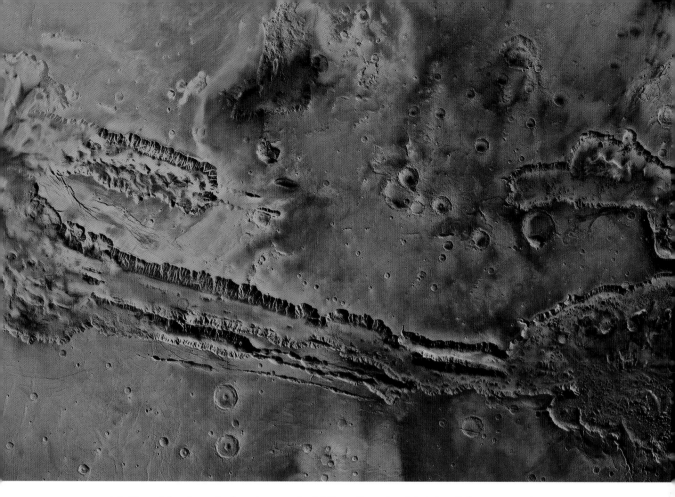

Valles Marineris is about 2,485 miles (4,000 km) long and 124 miles (200 km) wide. In some places, the canyon sinks 6 miles (10 km) deep. By comparison, Earth's Grand Canyon is 277 miles (446 km) long, 18 miles (29 km) at its widest, and in places 1 mile (1.6 km) deep.

Valles Marineris was discovered in the 1970s when NASA's Mariner 9 probe began orbiting Mars. Scientists have been searching for clues about how the canyon formed. Unlike the Grand Canyon, most of Valles Marineris wasn't created by water erosion. Instead, scientists think it was a crack that opened up billions of years ago as large volcanoes caused the nearby Tharsis region to bulge upward. Millions of years later, landslides and rushing floodwaters on Mars may have further widened the giant canyon.

OLYMPUS MONS

Olympus Mons is the largest volcano in the solar system. It is an extinct shield volcano, formed almost completely from lava flows. Viewed from the side, shield volcanos have a low profile, and resemble a warrior's shield. Hawaii's Mauna Kea is a famous shield volcano. Olympus Mons is about 100 times larger.

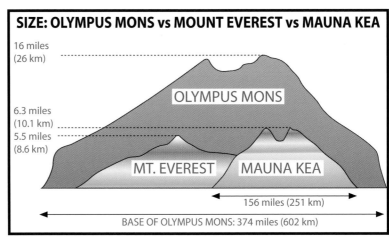

SIZE: OLYMPUS MONS vs MOUNT EVEREST vs MAUNA KEA

16 miles (26 km)

OLYMPUS MONS

6.3 miles (10.1 km)

5.5 miles (8.6 km)

MT. EVEREST   MAUNA KEA

156 miles (251 km)

BASE OF OLYMPUS MONS: 374 miles (602 km)

Olympus Mons is about the same size as Arizona.

Olympus Mons towers 16 miles (26 km) over the surrounding plains. The massive volcano has a diameter of 374 miles (602 km). That is about the same area as the state of Arizona.

Olympus Mons is in the volcanic Tharsis region. Scientists believe magma from the planet's interior pushed the planet's crust upward into a vast plateau. In some spots, the magma burst to the surface. Besides Olympus Mons, there are several other large volcanoes in this region. The three largest are southeast of Olympus Mons. They are Ascraeus Mons, Pavonis Mons, and Arsia Mons. (*Mons* is a Latin word that means mountain.) Together, they are called the Tharsis Montes. (*Montes* is the Latin plural of mons.)

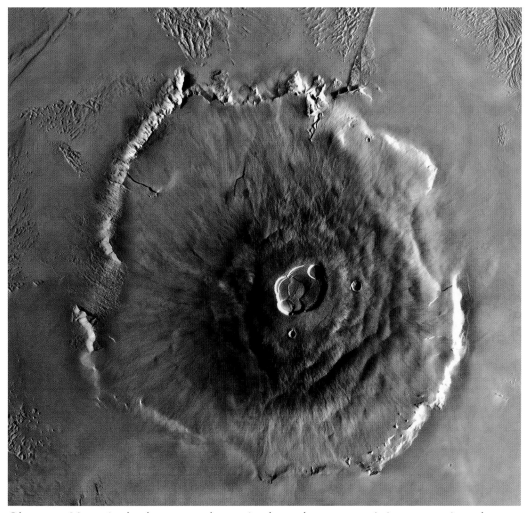

Olympus Mons is the largest volcano in the solar system. It is now extinct, but was formed when magma burst to the surface from Mars's interior.

Why are the volcanoes on Mars so much bigger than those on Earth? There are several possible reasons. The eruptions may have been more frequent. The lower gravity on Mars allowed the lava to spread out farther. Also, the Martian planetary crust isn't divided into huge plates that slowly move, like on Earth. On Mars, once magma burst to the surface, the lava kept building up for millions of years in the same spot.

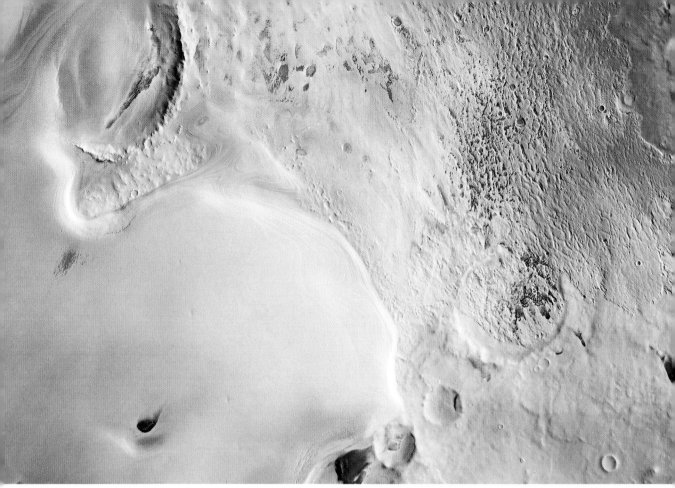

POLES

Above: A view of Promethei Planum in Mars's south pole region. The area is seasonally covered with a layer of ice more than 11,483 feet (3,500 m) thick.

Like Earth, Mars has a north pole and a south pole. They are large enough that they can be seen from Earth with telescopes. Each pole has a permanent cap of water ice that is several miles thick. If all the ice were to suddenly melt, it would flood the entire planet with water 33 feet (10 m) deep.

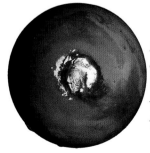

A view of Mars's North Pole from above the planet.

A view of Mars's South Pole from below the planet.

During each poles' winter, constant darkness descends and the landscape is plunged into severe cold. Carbon dioxide (CO_2) in the air freezes and falls to the ground as frost, snow, or thick fog. This "dry ice" is several yards thick. It makes up about 30 percent of the polar ice cap in winter. (The frozen CO_2 level at the south pole is much thicker in places.)

During the warmer, sunnier summer months, the frozen carbon dioxide thaws. It turns back into a gas and returns to the atmosphere. This process generates strong winds, creating vast dust storms. Some water vapor also escapes into the atmosphere, which forms wispy clouds that have been seen by NASA satellites. These same satellites observed that when either pole is plunged into winter, nearly 4 trillion tons (3.6 million metric tons) of carbon dioxide freezes out of the air.

CRATERS

There are hundreds of thousands of craters on Mars. They were caused by passing asteroids, meteoroids, or comets captured by Mars's gravity. When these objects slammed into the Martian surface, they created circular impact craters. Some are small, while others measure hundreds of miles across.

Why does Mars have so many more visible craters than Earth? The atmosphere on Mars is much thinner, which means most space objects do not burn up before reaching the surface.

Also, any impact craters that formed on Earth millions of years ago have been smoothed away by wind and rain erosion, or hidden by vegetation.

When you study a map of Mars, you may be surprised to see that most of the northern hemisphere is smooth, covered over by ancient lava flows. The south, on the other hand, is pockmarked by thousands of impact craters. How can this be? One theory is that a gigantic asteroid rivaling the size of Earth's Moon struck Mars billions of years ago. If true, it would make the northern part of Mars the site of the biggest impact crater ever seen.

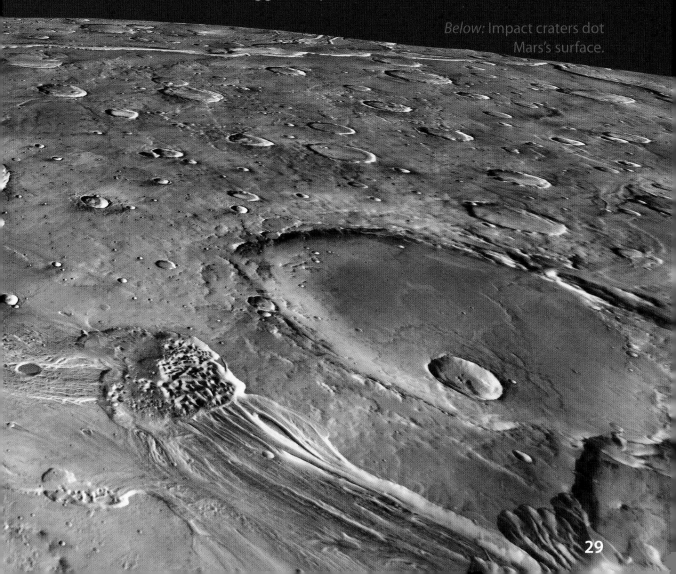

Below: Impact craters dot Mars's surface.

WATER ON MARS

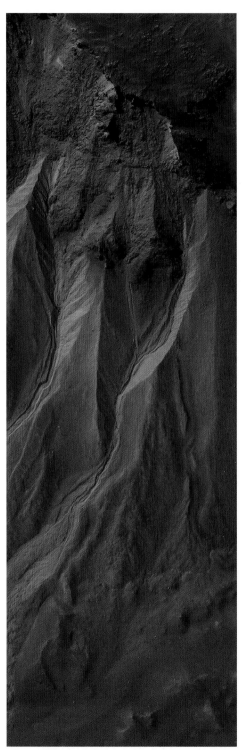

About 3.5 billion years ago, oceans and rivers of liquid water flowed freely on the surface of Mars. At that time, Mars was a warmer, wetter world. Evidence of this includes flow channels carved into the Martian rocks, deltas, lake beds, and river valleys. All of these have been seen by orbiting NASA satellites. On the surface, NASA rovers have found rocks and minerals that could only have formed with the help of liquid water.

Then, something happened to the ancient seas on Mars. The atmosphere became too thin, and water couldn't stay liquid any longer. Over billions of years, the water evaporated or froze, until Mars became the dry planet we see today.

Flow channels appear in the slopes of impact craters on Mars.

This illustration shows charged particles from a solar storm stripping away part of Mars's atmosphere. It is one of the processes of Martian atmosphere loss studied by NASA's MAVEN orbiter, beginning in 2014. Unlike Earth, Mars lacks a global magnetic field that could deflect charged particles coming from the Sun.

Where did the planet's liquid water go? Scientists are still trying to unravel the mystery, but there are strong clues. Billions of years ago, Mars's inner molten core cooled, and the planet lost its protective magnetic shield. For several billion years, energetic particles streaming from the Sun, called the solar wind, eroded Mars's atmosphere. On Earth, our strong magnetic shield protects the atmosphere by deflecting most of the solar wind. On Mars, much of the atmosphere was pushed into outer space. When the atmosphere became too thin, liquid water could no longer exist on the surface. It either froze or evaporated.

Not all of the water on Mars was lost to outer space. As the planet's atmosphere slowly thinned over millions of years, much of the water froze and collected at the poles, enough to flood the entire planet many feet deep if it ever melted.

Could some of the water have seeped under the surface of Mars? The answer appears to be yes. Using ground-penetrating radar and tests by NASA rovers, many scientists have concluded that a vast amount of water ice is trapped underground. One region in the northern plains may contain as much water as Lake Superior, the largest of the Great Lakes on Earth.

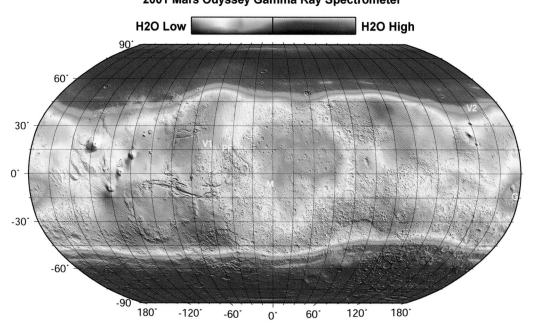

Map of Water on Mars
2001 Mars Odyssey Gamma Ray Spectrometer

This NASA map shows the relative amounts of water on Mars. Most of it, if not all, is water ice. The map shows that water is scarce near the equator, but more abundant at the north and south poles. Orbiting satellites were able to detect gamma rays from the Martian soil. Water has a unique gamma ray energy "signature." The map was created using this data.

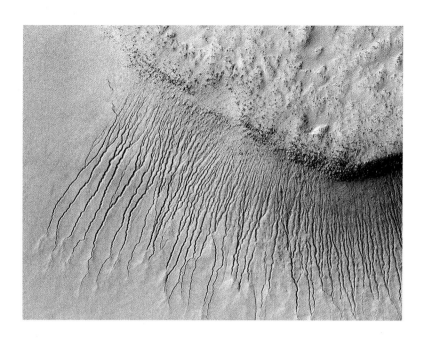

A detailed image of Mars's surface shows numerous gullies and ravines, ranging in width from 3 to 33 feet (1 to 10 m), flowing out from the side of an impact crater. Researchers are still trying to discover how the channels formed.

Other evidence of water on Mars includes bright material that is scattered on the landscape after fresh meteorite impacts. NASA satellites have watched as the exposed material, likely water ice, slowly vaporized in the thin Martian atmosphere. Ice has also been seen sheltered in the shady areas of large craters. It is also possible that seasonal dark streaks appearing on steep slopes may be caused by salty water seeping downward. Or, the streaks could simply be caused by dark sand rolling downhill. More investigation will be needed.

Why is the search for water so important? If life ever existed on Mars, it would probably have needed liquid water to survive. If scientists find pools of water under the Martian surface, perhaps some sort of simple microbial life survives to this day. More importantly for future Martian colonists, finding large amounts of water, either liquid or ice, will be important for growing plants, drinking, and possibly producing hydrogen for rocket fuel.

THE MOONS OF MARS

Unlike Earth, Mars has two moons, Phobos and Deimos. They are named after characters in ancient Greek mythology. Phobos means "fear" (where we get the word "phobia") and Deimos means "dread." Both characters traveled with their father, Ares, into battle. Ares was the ancient Greek god of war. The Romans called him Mars. It was the name given to the Red Planet. The moons were discovered by astronomer Asaph Hall in 1877.

Both of Mars's moons are tiny and shaped like lumpy potatoes. Phobos is the larger of the two moons. Its average diameter is about 13.8 miles (22 km). Deimos is smaller, just 7.7 miles (12.4 km) across. It is possible the two moons were once asteroids that were captured by Mars's gravity.

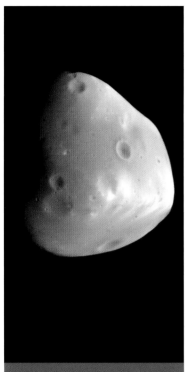

DEIMOS

PHOBOS

Deimos rises slowly in the east and sets in the west, just like Earth's Moon. Deimos has many craters, but appears smoother than its twin moon Phobos. Deimos orbits Mars about every 30 hours.

Phobos has many craters. Stickney Crater is 6 miles (10 km) in diameter, which is almost half the diameter of the moon itself! From the surface of Mars, Phobos appears to rise in the west and set in the east. Its orbit is low and fast. It circles the planet about twice each Martian day. Mars's gravity pulls Phobos closer and closer. In 30 to 50 million years, Phobos will either be pulled apart by Mars's gravity or crash into the planet's surface.

LIFE ON MARS?

Could there possibly be life on Mars? People have been asking that question about our close neighbor in the sky for hundreds of years. Four critical elements—carbon, oxygen, nitrogen, and hydrogen—are needed to support life as we know it. Mars has all of these elements today. We also know that in the planet's past, Mars had plenty of water to support whatever

A European Space Agency (ESA) mission, Mars Express Orbiter's goal is to examine the possibilities for past or present life on Mars. It will search for liquid water, which is essential for life as we understand it. Any liquid water that exists on Mars would be trapped underground where temperature and pressure could be sufficient to maintain its liquid state.

life forms may have arisen. Could we somehow detect those life forms, living or long dead? Perhaps there are fossils to be found among the Martian rocks. Now that NASA and other space agencies are sending sophisticated satellites and rovers to the Red Planet, we may someday soon find an answer.

There are certainly no plants or animals on the surface of Mars today. The atmosphere is too thin, and temperatures are far too cold. Also, without a thick atmosphere for protection, radiation from the Sun does long-term harm to any complex form of life. However, there is a chance that microscopic organisms could still be alive, perhaps left over from the planet's earlier, warmer days. Maybe someday we'll discover them in underground reservoirs of water, or some other sheltered place. Future missions to Mars will almost certainly continue looking for signs of life on the Red Planet.

There is a chance that microscopic organisms could still be found on Mars. Scientists continue to search for answers.

EXPLORING MARS

Mars is a world that has changed often during its long history. It has many features similar to Earth. Mars has seasons, volcanoes, weather, and canyons. It has polar ice caps, and was once home to oceans of liquid water. Unlike Earth, Mars has an atmosphere that is extremely thin, and it has a much weaker magnetic field. All these features make Mars a tempting place to study and explore.

Humans first began exploring Mars without ever leaving the safety of Earth. During ancient times, many cultures all over the world were aware of the mysterious Red Planet, including astronomers from Europe, China, India, and the Middle East. When telescopes became strong enough and widely available, some surface features came into view. They included the bright polar ice caps, and dark areas that seemed to grow during the planet's summers. Some people thought these dark areas could be forests.

Telescopes of Galileo Galilei.

In 1609, Galileo Galilei became the first person to observe Mars through a telescope. Today he is known as the father of modern astronomy.

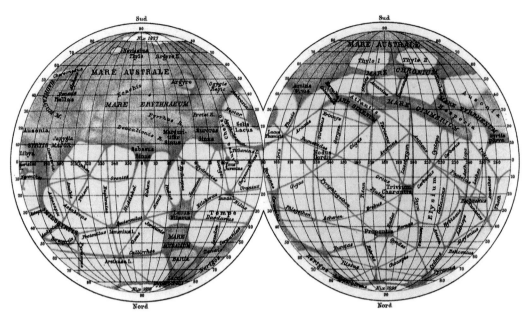

Giovanni Schiaparelli's map of Mars, created from 1877-1888. Many of his original place names are still used today.

In 1877, astronomer Giovanni Schiaparelli of Italy drew the first detailed map of the Red Planet. He noted long, straight lines on the surface, which he called *canali*. The word means "channels" in Italian, but many people thought Schiaparelli was describing canals dug by intelligent Martians. In the 1890s, American Percival Lowell and other astronomers also claimed to see canals on Mars. These observations were later found to be caused by optical illusions.

By the 1960s, Earth-based telescopes had reached their limit in exploring Mars. If we wanted to learn more, we would have to send spaceships to the Red Planet. In July 1965, NASA's Mariner 4 spacecraft zoomed past Mars. It sent back to Earth 22 images of the surface of the planet. The images shocked many people. Instead of oceans, forests, and canals, there was desert. Instead of cities, there were thousands of craters. Mars appeared to be a dead place, like the Moon.

In 1971, NASA's Mariner 9 probe arrived, becoming the first spacecraft to orbit an alien world. It took pictures that revealed giant volcanoes and a canyon 10 times bigger than the Grand Canyon. Most exciting of all was evidence of water in Mars's distant past.

Later in 1971, a pair of landers from the Soviet Union touched down on Mars, but they either crashed or failed shortly after landing. Then, in 1975, NASA's Viking 1 and Viking 2 landers safely arrived on the surface of Mars. They chemically analyzed soil samples and sent back high-resolution photos of the Martian landscape.

Mariner 4 was launched on November 28, 1964, and journeyed for 228 days to the Red Planet. It provided the first close-range images of Mars. A 'real-time data translator' machine converted Mariner 4 digital image data into numbers printed on strips of paper. Too anxious to wait for the official processed image, employees from the Voyager Telecommunications Section at NASA's Jet Propulsion Laboratory attached these strips side by side to a display panel and hand colored the numbers like a paint-by-numbers picture. In total, Mariner 4 produced 22 photographs showing lunar-type craters on a desert-like surface.

More missions followed the Viking landers, including high-tech orbiters and rovers. The spacecraft came not only from the United States, but also the Soviet Union, the European Space Agency, India, Japan, China, and Russia. Some spacecraft were successful, but many were not. Getting to Mars is hard, but scientists learn from their mistakes as well as their successes. We learn more after each mission.

Today, there are several spacecraft orbiting the Red Planet or roving across the Martian landscape. NASA's Opportunity and Curiosity rovers have lasted many years beyond their mission plans. All of these engineering marvels have given us a greater understanding of Mars. Yet, there are many mysteries to be solved.

A 2018 selfie by Curiosity. The rover is investigating a clay-rich slope on Mars's Vera Rubin Ridge.

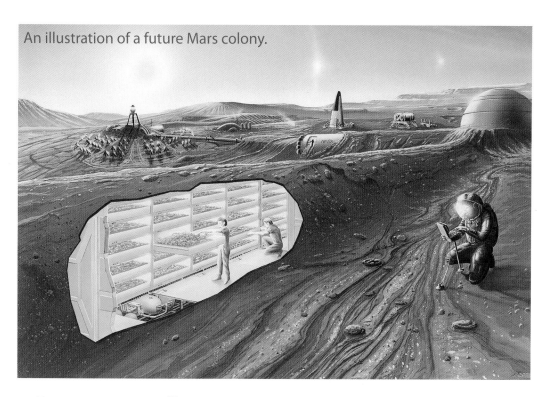

An illustration of a future Mars colony.

Future missions will continue to explore Mars's geology, its atmosphere, and whether it once harbored life. Probes and rovers, however, have their limits. NASA plans to send astronauts to Mars within the next two decades. Whether or not they meet that deadline, humans will someday most likely walk on Mars. They may even live in permanent colonies.

There will be many challenges. Future colonists will need spacesuits and pressurized homes to survive in the cold, oxygen-poor atmosphere. They will need a source of water, and shielding to protect against radiation from the Sun. They will have to grow their own food, and make their own fuel and electricity. These are major problems, but scientists believe they can be overcome. Perhaps someday, if people live on Mars long enough, a human baby, the first, true Martian, will be born on the Red Planet.

TIMELINE

July 14-15, 1965—Mariner 4 (USA) spacecraft, first successful flyby of Mars.

Nov. 14, 1971—Mariner 9 (USA) orbiter arrives at Mars. First United States spacecraft to orbit a planet other than Earth.

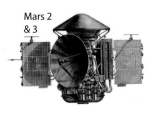

Nov. 27, 1971—Mars 2 (USSR) lander crashes. First human object to reach the surface of Mars.

Dec. 2, 1971—Mars 3 (USSR) lander successfully lands on Mars. Instruments fail 20 seconds after landing.

July 20, 1976—Viking 1 (USA) lander touches down on Mars. First lander to safely land on Mars and complete its mission.

Sept. 3, 1976—Viking 2 (USA) lander touches down on Mars.

Sept. 11, 1997—Mars Global Surveyor (USA) begins polar orbit around Mars and starts a nine-year mapping mission.

July 4, 1997—Mars Pathfinder (USA) lands successfully. Sojourner rover begins exploring Mars two days later.

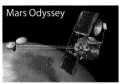
Mars Odyssey

Oct. 24, 2001—Mars Odyssey (USA) orbiter reaches Mars. Studies Mars's geology and radiation, and acts as communications relay for Martian rovers.

Mars Express

Dec. 25, 2003—Mars Express (European Space Agency) spacecraft enters Mars orbit. Accompanying Beagle 2 rover crashes on surface.

Spirit & Opportunity

Jan. 4, 2004—Spirit (USA) rover lands on Mars.

Jan. 24, 2004—Opportunity (USA) rover lands on Mars.

Mars Reconnaissance Orbiter

March 10, 2006—Mars Reconnaissance Orbiter (USA) reaches Mars.

Phoenix

May 25, 2008—Phoenix (USA) lander arrives at the Martian north pole, verifies presence of water ice.

Curiosity

August 6, 2012—Mars Science Laboratory (USA) rover, nicknamed Curiosity, lands on Mars.

MAVEN

Sept. 22, 2014—MAVEN (USA) orbiter reaches Mars and studies the Red Planet's upper atmosphere.

Mangalyaan

Sept. 24, 2014—Mars Orbiter Mission (India), also called *Mangalyaan* (Hindi for "Mars Craft"), reaches Mars and begins studying the planet's atmosphere. It is India's first mission to Mars.

ExoMars

Oct. 19, 2016—ExoMars Trace Gas Orbiter (joint European Space Agency and Roscosmos (Russia)) enters orbit around Mars. Lander crashes.

GLOSSARY

ASTEROID
A rocky object, smaller than a planet, that revolves around the Sun, usually between the orbits of Mars and Jupiter. Their size ranges from one to several hundred miles in diameter. Mars's two moons, Phobos and Deimos, are probably asteroids captured by the planet's gravitational pull millions of years ago.

EUROPEAN SPACE AGENCY (ESA)
A space agency, like NASA, that builds and flies spacecraft that explore the solar system. Its headquarters is in Paris, France. As of 2018, there are 22 countries that are members of the ESA.

METEOROID
A solid object, usually rocky, that moves through space. It is much smaller than an asteroid, ranging from the size of a grain of sand to about one meter in diameter. If a meteoroid enters a planet's atmosphere, it becomes a meteor. Earth's atmosphere is so thick that most meteors burn up, becoming streaks in the sky, which we call "falling" or "shooting stars." If a meteor survives and strikes the ground, it is called a meteorite.

NATIONAL AERONAUTICS AND SPACE ADMINISTRATION (NASA)
A United States government space agency started in 1958. NASA's goals include space exploration, as well as increasing people's understanding of Earth, our solar system, and the universe.

ORBIT
The circular path a moon or spacecraft makes when traveling around a planet or other large celestial body. There are several satellites orbiting Mars, including NASA's Mars Reconnaissance Orbiter and the European Space Agency's ExoMars Trace Gas Orbiter.

Probe

An unmanned space vehicle that is sent on missions that are too dangerous, or would take too long, for human astronauts to accomplish. Probes are equipped with many scientific instruments, like cameras and radiation detectors. Information from these instruments is radioed back to ground controllers on Earth.

Rover

A robotic vehicle that is driven over rough terrain by remote control.

Solar Wind

Streams of charged particles that are given off by stars. Solar wind is a plasma of electrons, protons, and other particles. They are so energetic they can escape from the Sun's gravity.

Soviet Union

A former country that included a union of Russia and several other communist republics. It was formed in 1922 and existed until 1991.

Telescope

A device to detect and observe distant objects by their reflection or emission of various kinds of electromagnetic radiation (like light). Most astronomy research today is conducted with telescopes that detect electromagnetic radiation other than visible light, such as radio or x-ray telescopes.

ONLINE RESOURCES

Booklinks
NONFICTION NETWORK
FREE! ONLINE NONFICTION RESOURCES

To learn more about Mars: the Red Planet, visit abdobooklinks.com. These links are routinely monitored and updated to provide the most current information available.

INDEX